WORKPLACE WARFARE:

A GUIDE TO OVERCOMING BATTLES ON THE JOB

BY COURTNI MICHELLE

PROFESSIONAL PUBLISHING MEETS POWERFUL PROMOTION

A wholly owned subsidary of TBN

DEDICATION

This book is dedicated to my late grandmother, Lavern Washington, and my aunts, Shelia Tyson and Sharon Fabre. From a very young age, these three ladies made sure that I attended church on a regular basis, which contributed to me developing a personal relationship with my Lord and Savior, Jesus Christ. I am forever grateful to them. Also, to my childhood pastor, Bishop James Quillen, who eloquently and consistently brought forth the Word of God to myself and many others. Lastly, to my friend, Warren Celestine, who hired me for my very first human resources role.

ACKNOWLEDGMENTS

First and foremost, I would like to acknowledge and thank God for providing me with the inspiration and motivation to write this book. Throughout my years of working in corporate America for several large firms, I have experienced and witnessed many situations that have proven to me that this book needed to be written. During my writing process, there were several instances when I questioned myself and my ability to complete this project. Every time those doubts entered my mind, God provided me with crystal clear confirmation that this is what He was calling me to do. I pray that my obedience to God serves as a blessing and resource to others.

TABLE OF CONTENTS

INTRODUCTION

For starters, this book was not written for the non-believers, fair-weather believers, or the doubters. This book was written for those who believe in the mighty power of our Lord and Savior, Jesus Christ. This book was written for those who trust that any obstacles in the workplace can be overcome with prayer and obedience to our Heavenly Father. If you have not yet accepted Jesus Christ as your personal Lord and Savior, I urge you to take a moment to do so. Open your Bible and go to the Book of Romans, chapter 10, verses 9 and 10.

> If you declare with your mouth, 'Jesus is Lord,' and believe in your heart that God raised him from the dead, you will be saved. For it is with your heart that you believe and are justified, and it is with your mouth that you profess your faith and are saved.
>
> **Romans 10:9–10 (NIV)**

The Holy Spirit initially gave me the idea to write this book in 2015. I began drafting an outline and writing notes on my electronic tablet. I slowly collected data over a three-year timeframe because I wanted to take my time with my book to make sure that it was perfect. Unfortunately, my tablet was stolen in early 2018, and all of my notes were lost. I was devastated, discouraged, and angry. I allowed my emotions to cloud my thoughts, and I concluded that it was not meant for me to write this book. Fast forward to late 2020. I was listening in on a prophetic call hosted by a world-renowned prophetess, and I received instruction to seek God and ask Him why did He allow certain things to happen in my life; specifically, what purpose He was grooming me for. I followed the instructions, and I prayed diligently for a few days so that I could hear clearly from God. After a few days had passed, the Holy Spirit revealed to me that I am in fact, supposed to write this book, but when I received the initial revelation in 2015, it was not time. I had not yet witnessed enough, gone through enough, and grown through enough workplace warfare in order for this book to make the impact that God intends for it to make. God then reminded me of the additional workplace warfare that I experienced after my tablet was stolen. Now I have increased faith, discernment, and spiritual eyes and obtained much more useful knowledge that I can share with the world, and for that, I am forever grateful.

Spiritual Warfare

In order to win in workplace warfare, it is necessary that you acknowledge the existence of spiritual warfare and have a general understanding of what it is.

For our struggle is not against flesh and blood, but against the rulers, against the authorities, against the powers of this dark world and against the spiritual forces of evil in the heavenly realms.

Ephesians 6:12 (NIV)

As the scripture tells us in Ephesians 6:12, our warfare is essentially against spiritual forces of evil. Once you decide to give your heart to Jesus, the enemy will do whatever he can to bring your heart back to sin and darkness. As a matter of fact, the enemy will ramp up his attacks once you decide to give your heart to Jesus.

Because your career is directly tied to your livelihood, workplace warfare is particularly draining to your mind, body, and soul. The enemy will proactively use people, events, circumstances, doubt, and even your own mind to attack you, distract you, and discourage you from following Jesus and essentially living out your God-given purpose.

Spiritual Eyes

Spiritual warfare is not personal. Since spiritual warfare is not personal, neither is workplace warfare personal. Many times, when we face any type of workplace battle, our immediate response is to take offense to the situation. Being that anger is a secondary emotion, according to healthypsych.

com, anger most oftentimes will follow your feelings of offense. This is a cycle that I want to encourage you to break.

When you begin to view people and situations through spiritual eyes versus viewing through your natural eyes, you begin to see them as the demonic spirits that are operating through them to accomplish the enemy's ultimate goal of dissuading you from following Jesus. Viewing people and situations with your spiritual eyes will also cause you to have increased stamina to battle and win in workplace warfare. How does one attain spiritual eyes? All you have to do is pray and ask God to give you spiritual eyes, and He will make it so.

Understand that experiencing anger and other similar emotions are a natural part of being human. With that said, it's okay to have emotions; just don't let the emotions have you. "If you become angry, do not let your anger lead you into sin, and do not stay angry all day" (Ephesians 4:26, GNT).

Throughout this book, I will take you on a journey where I will detail one of the toughest workplace battles that I have endured during the span of my entire corporate career. The battle that I will detail was intense and involved many moving parts, including an official internal investigation. As I detail my personal battle, I will provide revelation from what I learned during the battle and some additional revelation from a hindsight point of view. However, in the end, you will see that God proved Himself faithful, and I was vindicated.

In addition to reading the details of my personal workplace battle, you will also attain relative scriptures, practical tips, and strategies to help you endure and triumph in workplace warfare. Hypothetical examples and biblical perspectives are also provided.

My ultimate goal is to get you to do as we are instructed to do so in Proverbs 3:5–6 (NKJV), "Trust in the LORD with all your heart, And lean not on your own understanding; In all your ways acknowledge Him, And He shall direct your paths."

SECTION I:
THE BATTLE IS
IMMINENT

"There is a time for everything" (Ecclesiastes 3:1, NIV)

CHAPTER ONE

Workplace Politics

Warfare happens every day, all the time. Whether you believe it or not, you are in a battlefield. You are in warfare.

—Pedro Okoro

My very first human resources role was in a Shared Services Center for a Fortune 500 company in Louisiana. I mentally mapped out my future. I envisioned working my way up the corporate ladder, building an illustrious career, and subsequently retiring in my late 60s from this particular company. At that time, working for another organization was out of the question. As a proud employee, I showed up on time and rarely missed days. I was a fast learner with a high productivity rate. During my tenure in the Shared Services Center, I completed my Bachelor's degree and also a Master of Business Administration degree, both with concentrations in Human Resources Management. I was in my early 20s. I loved my company, and I loved my entry-level human resources role. I was also blessed to make several lifelong friends while serving in this role. Coming from humble beginnings, I was extremely proud of myself. My family and friends were proud of me as well.

Helping others is something that I have always enjoyed.

In my role within the Human Resources Shared Services Center, as a member of the leave of absence processing team, I was no different. I was a pretty routine employee. I would be one of the first to arrive each day. I would fix my coffee and then get to work. I would greet each of my coworkers as they filed in one after the other. My workplace personality can be classified as introverted, so I did not participate in much small talk throughout the day. When it was time for my lunch break, one of my favorite coworkers would send me an instant message, and we would have lunch together. At the end of each day, I would say good night to everyone as I exited the office and then head home.

I thought of myself as the ideal employee. I did not cause any trouble, and I did not want any trouble. No one can have an issue with an employee like that, right? *Wrong!* But little did I know, there was intense warfare on the horizon.

Workplace Politics Defined

Merriam-Webster defines workplace or office politics as "the activities, attitudes, or behaviors that are used to get or keep power or an advantage within a business or company."

First things first, there is some level of workplace politics that exists in every organization. Point. Blank. Period. One would be naïve to think otherwise. Observing and understanding your company's culture will help you understand the political environment of your workplace. Workplace politics can be negative or positive; however, since workplace politics is often paired with behaviors such as manipulation, bullying, or deception, negative workplace politics is most common; therefore, going forward, when I speak of workplace politics, I will be referring to the negative.

Workplace Politics Equals Workplace Warfare

Simply put, workplace politics equals workplace warfare.

Organizations are made up of individuals of diverse races, backgrounds, educational levels, ages, religions, and personal interests. Any individual can play host to a demonic spirit at any given time, and that fact alone makes the workplace a breeding ground for warfare. A political work environment can consist of a micromanaging boss, hypercompetitive teammates, or the cool clique. These are only just a few examples. Conflicting personalities types, differences of opinions, and personal motives are some of the perfect gateways for the enemy to come in and initiate warfare.

No One Is Exempt from Warfare

As Christians, we sometimes convince ourselves we should never have any issues in the workplace because we love God and choose to walk in love and faith. On the contrary, God's Word tells us in Matthew 5:45 (NKJV) that

"You may be sons of your Father in heaven; for He makes His sun rise on the evil and on the good, and sends rain on the just and on the unjust." With that said, it would be wise to remove the expectation that we will not experience workplace warfare because we have chosen to accept Jesus as our personal Lord and Savior.

Being involved in workplace politics is extremely difficult for those who just want to keep their heads down and perform their assigned roles to the best of their abilities; I am definitely one of those people. Due to that fact, I personally am not a fan of workplace politics, but I still acknowledge its existence in every organizational culture. While acknowledging the existence of workplace politics, I also continually make the decision to never compromise my spiritual and personal values.

Hypothetical Example

You are assigned to work on a project with one of your colleagues. As a team, you two decide to split the duties evenly. The project is completed and receives rave reviews from the manager. A few days later, you are informed by your manager that you and your colleague Tim will be presenting your project to the executive leadership team.

During the presentation, the executive leadership team was impressed by one particular portion of the project and asked for additional information. The impressive portion of the project is one of the duties that you completed. Before you could respond to the executive leadership's inquiry, Tim answered the question and took credit for your work. And just like that, the enemy has used your colleague Tim along with workplace politics to declare war on you.

Did the actions of your colleague upset you? That should not come as a surprise to anyone. Although you may be angry that Tim stole the credit for your work on the project, I want you to remember two things:

1. The blessings that God has specifically designed for you will be presented to you in His perfect timing.

2. God shall not be mocked, and He will not allow anyone to do you wrong and escape His wrath. (Refer to Galatians 6:7.)

Led by a personal desire to quickly climb the corporate ladder at any cost, Tim provided the perfect entryway for the enemy. As a result, he stole the credit for your work in hopes of obtaining favor from the executive leadership team while simultaneously committing a sin against God.

A harsh reality hit Tim very soon after his actions. When he signed off on the project documents and certified with his signature that he completed portions of the project that he truly did not complete, he falsified company documents. Falsifying documents is a violation of the company's code of conduct, and as a result, Tim's employment was terminated.

Biblical Perspective

This example brings me to reflect upon a story in the Bible that begins in Genesis chapter 27. Jacob deceived his father, Isaac, in order to steal the blessing that his father intended for his older brother, Esau. Esau was rightfully devastated when he found out what his brother had done, and then he began to plot to kill Jacob. Jacob escaped Esau, but he could not escape the wrath of God.

In Genesis chapter 29, Jacob was himself deceived by Laban and was forced to marry Leah, a woman he was not attracted to and did not want to marry. Later on in Genesis chapter 37, the Bible details how Jacob's favorite son, Joseph, was sold into slavery, but Jacob was told that he was killed by a wild animal. This news caused Jacob to mourn for many years.

On the other hand, we learn in Genesis chapters 32 and 33 Esau became successful in spite of what his brother Jacob had stolen from him. I am pretty sure that if Esau had gone against God and killed Jacob, he too would have spent many years dealing with the wrath of God.

Battle Summary

In the above example, your colleague Tim may have thought that stealing credit for your work would give him an advantage in the workplace; however, just like Jacob, he did not realize that his deception would bring about the wrath of God into his life. You are human, so it is only natural for you to have wanted to oust Tim and bring him to shame, but in some cases, it is best to just be still and know. As children of God, it is important to always take heed to Deuteronomy 32:35 (NKJV), where God tells us that "Vengeance is Mine," and fully trust that He will provide repayment for all wrongdoings.

Workplace Warfare Tips

- Accept that there are workplace politics in all organizations.

- Acknowledge that vengeance belongs to God.

- Never compromise your spiritual values.

A Scripture to Ponder

> "The righteous person may have many troubles, but the LORD delivers him from them all" (Psalm 34:19, NIV).

CHAPTER TWO

Spiritual Attacks Are Designed to Distract

Be aware when distractions come your way. You'll know it's a distraction when you stop doing what you're supposed to be doing and find yourself pondering things that have no value.

—Beverly R. Imes

It was now approximately one and a half years since I had begun working in the Human Resources Shared Services Center. My work routine had been the same, except now I had been given additional duties that included training others and working on cross-functional teams. However, by this time, I had now identified the office gossips and pot-stirrers. I tried my best to stay out of their way. The cohesiveness of our team went downhill drastically when one particular pot-stirrer was promoted to a role on my team. I will refer to her as the queen pot-stirrer. Her spirit reeked of drama and divisiveness. I recall during my very first week of working in the Human Resources Shared Services Center, the queen pot-stirrer cornered me in the breakroom and asked me outright, "So, have you figured out who you like and don't like yet?" She was referring to my colleagues on my team as well as the others in the department. I knew at that moment that she was trouble and that I should stay far away from her. What made things worse is that she easily influenced the other pot-stirrers. She had so many people fooled, but she did not fool my discernment.

Although I tried to stay out of their way, the drama always found its way to me. For example, because I participated in very little small talk, the pot-stirrers always made assumptions and started rumors that I was angry about one thing or another. What they failed to realize was that I had an introverted workplace personality. The more I was subjected to the daily rumors and microaggressions that I had to endure from the pot-stirrers, the job, and the position that I once loved and looked forward to going to, the more I slowly began to hate ad dread going to.

During my tenure in the Human Resources Shared Services Center, I would work all day and then go home and complete work towards my Bachelor's degree and Master's degree programs. I say that to demonstrate that I had very long days. The stress from work soon began to affect my ability to concentrate on my collegiate studies.

I remember as I would drive to work in the mornings, I would ride in silence so that I could pray and ask God to allow me to have a good day. The stress from work started affecting my mental and physical health. I would experience panic attacks during the workday and sleeplessness at night.

That was truly a rough time period for me.

Now that I have grown professionally and I am now more mature in my walk with Christ, I now can look back at that situation and see it exactly for what it was: workplace warfare. The enemy was operating in those coworkers to attack and distract me from fulfilling my God-given purpose.

Everyone Has a Specific Purpose

Purpose, that is what we were all created for! Each and every one of you is born with a God-given purpose. The purpose and plans that God has for your life are "to prosper you and not to harm you," as stated in Jeremiah 29:11 (NIV). Although the Bible says that His plan is to prosper you, your God-given purpose is far greater than your own personal desires. Your purpose is ultimately designed to show God's glory to the world, all while He uses you as a vessel. When God can show His glory through you, others will be drawn to Him. How do you find out what your God-given purpose is? It's actually not that difficult; all you have to do is seek God through prayer, fasting, and meditation, and God will certainly reveal your purpose to you.

Now that I have given you some background on purpose, unfortunately, I now have to disappoint you by telling you that the enemy is willing to do anything and everything he can do to prevent you from fulfilling God's purpose for your life. As stated in John 10:10 (NIV), the enemy "comes only to steal, kill, and destroy." In the workplace, the enemy wants to steal your creativity, kill your confidence, and destroy your relationships. Distraction is a method that the enemy often uses to accomplish his goals. When you are distracted, your attention is temporarily diverted from God and your purpose. If we fall prey to the enemy's distractions, our faith also becomes ineffective because we tend to exalt the distraction and not God.

Can you prevent the enemy from attempting to distract you? No, you cannot, but the good news is that you can learn to easily recognize distractions. In order to easily recognize distractions, you should always expect distractions. In 1 Peter 5:8 (NIV), it says, "Be alert and of sober mind. Your enemy the devil prowls around like a roaring lion looking for someone to devour."

Jealousy and Envy

Jealousy and envy are popular tools that the enemy uses to distract you and initiate workplace warfare. Many of you may think of jealousy and envy as one and the same, but in actuality, they are some distinctions between these two emotions. Jealousy is the fear of losing something that you already have, and envy is wanting something that someone else has. An example of jealousy in the workplace is when your boss starts assigning higher-level assignments to you, and your coworker, who is a team lead, then begins to experience negative emotions out of fear that you will be given their role as a team lead. An example of envy in the workplace is when you and a coworker interview for the same promotion. You are ultimately selected for the role, and your coworker then begins to experience negative emotions because they were not selected.

Additionally, understand that jealousy and envy are not always tied to the tangible. Your positive personality and the way that others are drawn to you can cause some people in the workplace to become jealous or envious of you. Although there are some distinctions between jealousy and envy, these two emotions are frequently coupled together.

When the spirit of jealousy and envy takes root in someone within the workplace, warfare becomes inevitable. James 3:16 (NLT) states, "For wherever there is jealousy and selfish ambition, there you will find disorder and evil of every kind." What the Bible tells us of jealousy and envy is true. Albeit quite normal for anyone to feel the unpleasant emotions of jealousy or envy at any given time, it is the actions that follow those uncontrolled feelings that bring about the disorder and evil.

Hypothetical Example

Let's expand upon the jealousy and envy hypothetical example that I mentioned earlier:

Recently there was an internal position posted for your department. This role would be considered a promotion because your job duties would expand and your salary would increase significantly. You immediately felt that you would be a good fit for the role. So naturally, you prayed about it and asked God for confirmation on if you should apply for the role. Once you received your heavenly confirmation, you submitted your application. The selection process for this role was extremely competitive. The final decision was down to you and Nina, another highly qualified candidate who others in the department often referred to as the "unofficial team lead." After a successful second-round interview process, you were eventually selected for the promotion instead of Nina. The hiring manager provided feedback to Nina as to why she was not selected and what she could do to improve and possibly be selected for a future promotion.

When the announcement was made to the department that you were the selected candidate, Nina instantly became envious because she thought that she was the most qualified candidate due to her having several more years of experience than you. Nina also began to experience feelings of jealousy because she assumed that now the other teammates in the department would refer to you as the "unofficial team lead." Those feelings of jealousy and envy that Nina was experiencing quickly evolved into unprovoked contempt towards you. Nina then decided that she would sabotage and undermine you wherever there was an opportunity in hopes of demonstrating to the leadership team that she should have been the chosen candidate for the role that you were selected for.

With that decision being led by feelings of jealousy and envy, Nina has subconsciously agreed to play host to those evil spirits; and at that moment, workplace warfare has been declared.

One of your first duties in your new role is to lead a highly visible cross-functional project team. Nina has been assigned to be a member of the team. As the leader of the project team, it is your responsibility to plan the scope of the project and to assign roles to members of the team. You also are required to conduct status update meetings on a regular basis.

During your project team meetings, you have noticed that Nina's disposition towards you has changed. Her attitude is no longer warm and friendly; it is now distant and cold. In addition to being distant and cold, Nina frequently interrupts you when you're speaking and exhibits disruptive and unprofessional behavior such as mumbling under her breath and rolling her eyes while you speak, all in an effort to make it appear that you are not capable of leading the team. What is unsettling and hurtful is that you have observed that Nina's unprofessional behavior is only directed towards you. Coupled with the negative behaviors, the quality of the work that Nina has been submitting has also been subpar. The subpar submissions have caused you to have to make many time-consuming corrections to her assignments.

You are rightfully stressed at this point because this is an important project for the company.

Being that it is your goal to perform well in your role as a project team lead, you would prefer to resolve the conflict without management intervention. However, your requests to meet with Nina one-on-one to discuss your recent interactions are ignored. It is not your goal to get Nina into any trouble, but all of your efforts thus far have been unsuccessful. At this point, you have no other choice but to take your concerns to management.

While meeting with your manager in regards to your concerns with Nina, you were informed that several other members of the project team have already submitted complaints. As a result of the complaints, Nina will face disciplinary action and will be removed from the project team.

Biblical Perspective

The enemy has used the evil spirits of jealousy and envy to influence sin since the beginning of time. One of the first instances in the Bible of jealousy and envy influencing sin is the story of the brothers Cain and Abel in Genesis chapter 4. Both brothers worked the land and provided offerings to the Lord. Abel's offering was accepted by the Lord, but Cain's offering was not. An anger-filled Cain then became jealous of his brother Abel, and as a result of the jealousy, Cain killed Abel.

Prior to killing Abel, the Lord instructed Cain on what he should do in order to have his offerings accepted. Instead of following the Lord's instructions and making the necessary corrections, Cain allowed the evil spirits of jealousy and envy to influence him to lure his brother Abel into a field and kill him. In this particular instance, the evil spirits of jealousy and envy accomplished the enemy's goal of distracting Cain. Because Cain was distracted, he failed to listen to the Lord's constructive feedback. Cain also did not yield to the Lord's warning as described in Genesis 4:7,

> You will be accepted if you do what is right. But if you refuse to do what is right, then watch out! Sin is crouching at the door, eager to control you. But you must subdue it and be its master.

Genesis 4:7 (NLT)

As a consequence of his brother's murder, Cain received a lifetime punishment. He was banished from Eden, declared a homeless wanderer, and the fields that he cultivated would no longer produce any crops no matter how hard he worked. I am certain that had Cain known what his punishment would be, he would not have killed Abel.

Battle Summary

Similar to Cain, Nina too allowed the spirits of jealousy and envy to influence her to commit sin. In both cases, each person deliberately formulated a plan to cause harm to another person. When you read the Book of Proverbs, chapter 6 describes several acts that are detestable to the Lord. Specifically, verse 18, which states that the Lord hates *a heart that devises wicked schemes*. So, as a result of their actions, both experienced God's judgment and consequences.

Warfare is intended to make you weary and to make you doubt God. Although Nina may have gotten what she deserved in the end, her consequences do not negate the fact that the warfare was unprovoked, stressful, and draining. I totally understand, but as followers of Christ, I implore you not to allow the attack to cause you to sin in retaliation. Always keep in mind that the battle is a distraction. Go to God in prayer and ask Him to reveal what this attack is trying to distract you from. Also, ask God to help you manage your emotions while you are under attack. Last but not least, I urge you to "Put on the full armor of God, so that you can take your stand against the devil's schemes" (Ephesians 6:11, NIV). Stand firm in your faith and always put your trust in God.

Workplace Warfare Tips

- Expecting distractions is a defense against distractions.

- Uncontrolled emotions are an entryway for the enemy.

- Do not allow the weariness to cause you to doubt God.

A Scripture to Ponder

> "Cast your cares on the LORD and he will sustain you; he will never let the righteous be shaken" (Psalm 55:22, NIV).

CHAPTER THREE

Choose Your Battles Wisely

*Fight your battles through prayer, and win your
battles through faith.*

—Luffina Lourduraj

The attacks from the office pot-stirrers were growing more frequent and more intense as each day passed. Not only were the attacks more frequent and intense, but they also began to be pettier and more asinine. I found myself having to defend myself against the most minuscule accusations.

I recall after one of our weekly team meetings, one of the pot-stirrers came to me and asked to meet with me. I stopped what I was doing and followed her outside. Once the two of us were alone, the conversation went as follows:

Pot-stirrer: Are you mad at me about something?

Me: No, why do you think that I am mad at you?

Pot-stirrer: Well, during the staff meeting, you didn't look at me.

Me: I'm sorry, I did not know that looking at you was a requirement; but no, I am not mad at you about anything.

I then proceeded back inside the building to get back to work. I can distinctly remember shaking my head and feeling so annoyed by that conversation.

A few days later, I received a meeting request from my supervisor. I had no idea what the meeting was in reference to. Much to my chagrin, the meeting was in reference to the conversation that I had a few days prior with one of the pot-stirrers. During the meeting, my supervisor proceeded to tell me the exaggerated version of the conversation that was told to her by the pot-stirrer. My supervisor then went on to say that my entire team thinks that I am unapproachable, which I knew was false. I knew that to be false because I had genuine friendships outside of work with two of my teammates.

For the sake of full transparency, I must admit that I had grown weary, and my spirit was weakening. As my spirit was weakening, my prayer life was beginning to weaken as well. The enemy had me exactly where he wanted me, in a weakened and battle fatigued state.

Due to my battle fatigue, I began to react to the warfare in my flesh. I began to respond to false accusations with long emails laced with negative tones. I would schedule meetings with the department manager demanding a discussion to hear my side of the story. Although I had facts and evidence to disprove the accusations, nothing was being done to address the pot-stirrers' behavior. I was fighting too many battles at one time. The more I attempted to defend myself, the more the gang of pot-stirrers would attack. At this point, I was miserable. I did not know who I could trust on my team. I now felt like an outcast on a team that I had once loved.

Hindsight Perspective

When you attempt to fight spiritual warfare with fleshly weapons, you will undoubtedly receive fleshly results in return. Anger, anxiety, fatigue, and depression are all examples of fleshy results when you choose to fight battles in your own strength. It is not God's will for you to live in a constant state of frustration. Although it is easier said than done, when faced with workplace warfare, you must remember what Romans 8:31 (KJV) says, "If God be for us, who can be against us?"

As I look back on my personal workplace battle, I now realize that there were plenty of opportunities for me to stand still and allow God to fight my battles. There were also many opportunities for me to pause and ask God which battle should I fight. In all honesty, I did not consult with God as much as I should have. Yes, I was consistently praying for God to deliver me from the battle, but I was not taking time to seek Him for strategy. Along with asking for strategy, I should have also asked God to help me govern my emotions because our emotions can sometimes overpower our intelligence if we allow them to.

Seeking God during workplace warfare is so important because while He is doing what only He can do in the spiritual realm, He will simultaneously provide us with strategy and favor to operate in the natural realm.

Biblical Perspective

Many times, when we are faced with warfare, the enemy distracts us with our own emotions, so we then begin to focus on the circumstances in the natural and consequently forget that the God that we serve operates in the supernatural. This is proven in the Book of Judges with the story of Gideon.

In the Book of Judges, chapter 6, the Israelites were in captivity by the Midianites and were experiencing immense suffering. God sent an angel to tell an Israelite judge named Gideon that he was the chosen one to rescue Israel from the hands of the Midianites. Being that Gideon was not a mighty warrior and he, in fact, considered himself a weakling, it was hard for him to grasp the fact that God was choosing him to do such a great task. Gideon was so afraid that although God told him in Judges 6:16 (NLT), "I will be with you. And you will destroy the Midianites as if you were fighting against one man," he continued to ask God for several signs so that he can be certain that he was the man for the job.

After Gideon was satisfied with the signs that God provided and the proof that he was indeed the chosen person to rescue the Israelites from the Midianites, Gideon began to prepare an army of 32,000 men for battle. Because God is the awesome and amazing God that He is, He made Gideon trim his army down to just 300 men! At that point, Gideon's fear was beginning to make him focus on the natural battle instead of resting on the fact that a supernatural God has assured him that he will not be defeated and that he will not be killed. God's reasoning behind shrinking the army was to show the Israelites that their victory would not be because of their own strength. After one final confirmation from God, Gideon and the Israelite army went on to defeat the Midianites just as God told him that he would.

Battle Summary

When some people read the story of Gideon, they often view him as foolish because he asked so many follow-up questions after God initially spoke to him. I, however, view Gideon as wise. Yes, he was afraid, but most people are fearful when faced with the unknown. Gideon was wise in my eyes because he did not allow his fear to prevent him from consulting with God.

Had I consulted God for strategy during my personal battle, I am certain that I would not have endured so much misery and mental anguish. In addition to seeking and consulting God, I should have fully trusted God with the outcome. Completely trusting God with the outcome allows you to rest and have peace in the midst of your battles.

Workplace Warfare Tips

- Always consult with God before you act.

- Trusting God with the outcome generates peace.

A Scripture to Ponder

> "Fear not, for I *am* with you; Be not dismayed, for I *am* your God. I will strengthen you, Yes, I will help you, I will uphold you with My righteous right hand" (Isaiah 41:10, NKJV).

Chapter Four

Always Try to Represent the Kingdom

The beginning of anxiety is the end of faith, and
the beginning of true faith is the end of anxiety.

—George Muller

As the days, weeks, and months went on, I had become a shell of a person. The internal fire that used to burn so vehemently within me for the work that I was assigned to do was now barely a spark. As much as we would like to think that we can easily separate our work life from our home life, I learned that that is not always the case. All of my close friends and family members were aware of the troubles that I was experiencing on my job. I was on a never-ending emotional rollercoaster that I desperately wanted to exit. Due to workplace warfare, irritability had become a frequent and prominent emotion. I was always bothered and on edge.

I soon learned that when you are in a constant state of irritability, you can sometimes wound an innocent bystander.

In an earlier chapter, I mentioned that I had been given additional duties that included training because I had been deemed a subject matter expert on the newly installed employee time-keeping system. One day, one of my teammates, whom I did not consider a pot-stirrer, came over to my desk to ask me a question. The question that she asked me was the same question that she had asked me numerous times before, and for some reason, she was not retaining the information that I had shared with her on several occasions. Before I realized what I was doing, I yelled at her and said something to the effect of, "Why are you not getting this in your head?" As soon as the words left my mouth, I was immediately remorseful. This particular teammate was sadly a victim of my misguided energy. I apologized to her a short while later because my conscience would not allow me to go on without doing so. However, what I did not know is that with my actions in my moment of frustration, I provided the pot-stirrers with a green light to initiate their fiercest attack against me.

Representing the Kingdom

In the Book of Corinthians, it says, "So we are Christ's ambassadors; God is making His appeal through us" (2 Corinthians 5:20, NLT). Let's define the term ambassador. Merriam-Webster defines "ambassador" as "an authorized representative or messenger." With that said, it is clear that the Bible instructs us to represent Christ to those around us. Do not be mistaken; this Bible verse is not demanding perfection once you accept Jesus as your personal Lord and Savior; this verse is letting you know that you have an opportunity to represent Jesus so well in your day-to-day life that others would want to get to know Him for themselves. Whether you realize it or not, others are constantly watching you to observe how you carry yourself, especially during adversarial times, so representing the kingdom of God is an important task. The quote by William J. Toms now comes to mind, "Be careful how you live; you may be the only Bible some people ever read."

I know you may now be thinking that the task of representing the kingdom of God may be a difficult challenge. What if I told you that once you make the decision to become a follower of Jesus Christ, you will have immediate access to all of the benefits that the kingdom of God has to offer, such as peace, forgiveness, and redemption? This is true. I am basically telling you that God will provide you with the tools that you need to represent His kingdom. I would like to remind you again that God is not looking for perfection; He just wants you to try to be the best representative that you can be. Refer back to the name of this chapter, "Always Try to Represent the Kingdom." With that said, I ask you to not get hung up on how difficult it may be for you to represent the kingdom; instead, shift your focus on the awesomeness of the Creator of the kingdom. In the words of my late grandmother, "Nothing beats a failure except a try."

Anger Is a Tricky Emotion

I urge you to be very careful when you become angry

because anger is a very tricky emotion. Anger is a tricky emotion because although it is a normal emotion, it can also be used as an entryway for demonic spirits to come in and operate in your life. So again, yes, you will still experience negative emotions such as anger from time to time, but when Jesus lives in your heart, the emotions will not overcome you and cause you to sin.

Anytime the enemy can use warfare to attack you, make you angry, and then, as a result, you act in any manner that is contrary to your godly countenance, then that is, of course, a win for Satan and his demonic underworld. But let me reaffirm to you that experiencing anger is quite normal. In fact, there are several instances in the Bible where Jesus Himself became angry; however, Jesus did not sin as a result of His anger, and that is the key.

Exercising Self-Control

In the Book of Galatians, chapter 5, Apostle Paul introduced us to the fruit of Spirit. The "fruit" of the Spirit is the foundational characteristic of a Christian lifestyle. There is nine total, one of them being self-control. Self-control is the ability to live your life with appropriate restraints. Some people would rather God control us and make us do what is right, but we are not robots. God gave man free will, so exercising self-control is our individual responsibility. Exhibiting self-control in your day-to-day lives is no easy feat, but by practicing self-control, you increase your ability to demonstrate self-control in the future when the need arises. I agree with Joyce Meyer when she says, "It (self-control) develops as we spend time fellowshipping with God and practicing obedience to Him." The keyword in Joyce's quote is *obedience*. Obedience to God is a building block for developing self-control.

Hypothetical Example

You have been a subject matter expert for a major corporation for approximately ten years. You recently decided that in order to advance your career, it would be beneficial for you to obtain some additional skillsets by spending more time in your company's manufacturing plants. After speaking to your boss about your career goals, you were given a one-year field assignment.

On the first day of your new field assignment, you arrived early so that you could familiarize yourself with the building and also set up your office space. At the facility's morning meeting, you were allowed to introduce yourself to the local staff that you would be directly working with for the next year. You received a warm welcome which made you instantly conclude that your next year of working in a manufacturing plant would be a pleasant one.

After your first few days onsite, you now have your office set up just the way you want it. You have several Bible scriptures and pictures of your family proudly posted. One day while on your way to the breakroom, you overheard a conversation amongst several of your coworkers, and you were the topic. Specifically, you overheard your colleague Jim saying some extremely offensive comments in regards to you displaying your Christianity in the workplace. You were immediately offended, then a moment later, you were angry. Your first instinct was to walk into the breakroom and confront Jim, but instead, you turned around and proceeded back to your office. Once in your office with the door closed, you begin to pray. You thought about what Proverbs 16:32 (NKJV) says, "*He who is* slow to anger *is* better than the mighty, And he who rules his spirit than he who takes a city.*"* After a few minutes of prayer and meditation, the anger subsided, but you also knew that the issue still had to be addressed.

Early the next morning, you saw Jim in his office, and you asked him if the two of you could speak privately for a moment. As you begin to reveal that you overheard his breakroom comments from the previous day, Jim's face became clearly blanched. You then assured Jim that you did not come with adversarial intentions. At that moment, Jim relaxed. You explained to Jim: "I display my Bible verses in my office so that I can instantly find comfort in God's Word when I need to. As a follower of Christ, it is important for me to respect others and their boundaries. Attempting to force my beliefs on you or anyone else is not something that I plan on doing. However, if you ever decide in the future that you would like to know more about Jesus, I would be more than happy to talk to you."

After you finished speaking, Jim was clearly remorseful and offered several sincere apologies. You then told Jim that you accepted his apologies, and you exited his office. Your working relationship with Jim from that day forward was a positive one.

Biblical Perspective

Life's trials and tribulations are a perfect opportunity to exercise self-control. In the Book of Job, the Bible details the story of a righteous God-fearing man bearing the same name. Not only was Job a righteous man, but he was also an extremely wealthy man with a loving family that consisted of his wife and ten children.

One day Satan suggested to God that Job only loved Him because of his many blessings. Satan then went on to say that if God took away all of Job's blessings, he would then surely curse God. God knew what Satan was saying was not true, so He allowed Satan to test Job. The only stipulation was that Satan was not allowed to lay a finger on Job himself.

Job soon experienced a series of unfortunate events. First, all of Job's livestock was stolen or killed. After that, all of Job's servants were killed. Next and most significantly, all ten of Job's children were killed in a storm. Lastly, Job was stricken with painful sores from the top of his head all the way to the soles of his feet. In addition to Job's misfortunes, Job's wife tried to convince him to curse God. Three of Job's closest friends were convinced that Job must have sinned in order to experience losses of this magnitude, and they insisted that Job repented when he had done nothing wrong.

Any of these tragedies alone would make the average person doubt God, but imagine having to cope with the combination of tragic events. Insufferable is the first word that comes to my mind.

At this point, you may be wondering how does the story of Job correlate with exercising self-control; well, let me explain. With all of the loss that Job experienced, it took self-control to not lose his faith and curse God. With all of the pressure that Job faced from those closest to him, it took self-control to not fold and give in to the opinions of others. When Job was suffering from his own illness, it took self-control to choose to trust God's plan instead of leaning to his own understanding.

Every test that Satan presented, Job successfully passed. The Bible says in Job chapter 42:10 (NIV), "After Job had prayed for his friends, the LORD restored his fortunes and gave him twice as much as he had before." The final chapter of the Book of Job goes on to say that Job also had ten more children and that his latter days were greater than his former days.

Battle Summary

When I reflect on the moment of frustration that I described in my personal battle, the hypothetical example, and the biblical examples from this chapter, there is one recurring theme; exercising self-control requires obedience to the Holy Spirit. Self-control requires you to deny your flesh of some sort of satisfaction. In these examples, satisfaction is any response that is contradictory to your godly countenance. In Luke 9:23 (NIV), the Bible says, "Whoever wants to be my disciple must deny themselves and take up their cross daily and follow me." In a nutshell, as a follower of Jesus, you must say "no" to yourself and "yes" to Christ. Always remember that exercising self-control is a form of worship.

Workplace Warfare Tips

- Anger is normal but can also initiate warfare.

- When you choose to follow Christ, you must strive to act like Him.

- Pausing to pray can change your day.

A Scripture to Ponder

"Consider it pure joy, my brothers and sisters, whenever you face trials of many kinds, because you know that the testing of your faith produces perseverance" (James 1:2–3, NIV).

Section II:
The Battle Is
Upon Us

"And everyone assembled here will know that
the Lord *rescues his people*" (1 Samuel 17:47, NLT).

CHAPTER FIVE

Under Attack Yet Covered by the Blood

*The battle belongs to the Lord, and we already
know that He wins the war.*

—**Jared Brock**

It was a typical busy day in the Human Resources Services Center. In fact, it was so busy that I failed to notice that two members of the corporate internal investigations team were onsite that day. I was so inundated and preoccupied with my assigned duties that I also failed to notice that members of my team were being called in to meet with the visiting corporate internal investigations team members one by one.

The last person that was interviewed by the internal investigations team was my team member, who was also a close personal friend of mine outside of work. When he returned to his desk, he sent me a text to inform me that the corporate investigations team was there to investigate a complaint against me! When I read the text, I immediately froze, and time seemed to stand still momentarily. Because of my knowledge of how internal investigations worked, I knew that I would be interviewing with the investigations team soon. My mind began to race. I then responded to his text and asked him if he knew what the specific complaint was in regards to. My friend did not know the specific complaint, but he immediately let me know that the investigators asked questions about the team personality dynamics, the pot-stirrers, and me. He then assured me that he was truthful with the investigators and that he had my back. His words were comforting, but anxiety still began to build in my body. Although I knew that I had not violated any company policies, I was still nervous because I had no idea what the specific complaint was and what I would have to ultimately defend myself against.

I sat nervously in my cubicle, waiting for my desk phone to ring with the investigators on the other line instructing me to come into the conference room. To my surprise, I looked up, and the two investigators were heading out of the door for their lunch break. I then decided to take my lunch break at that time as well so that I could go to my car and pray in private. Once I was in my car, I began to pray and ask God to cover me and see me through this investigation. After I finished praying, I called a trusted friend who worked in another department. She also prayed for me and provided me with some much-needed godly words of encouragement. At that moment, I knew that I was covered by the Blood of Christ and well equipped to handle whatever was about to be thrown my way.

After my lunch break was over, I went back to my cubicle to wait on the imminent phone call from the internal investigators. My desk phone rang shortly after I returned to my workstation, as I expected. I took a deep breath before I reached for the receiver. On the other end of the phone line was one of the internal investigators instructing me to come to speak with them in a conference room across the hall. When I arrived at the conference room, the two investigators were seated at a small round table. I sat down in the empty chair located in the center.

The meeting began with the two investigators introducing themselves. The lead investigator stated that he would be asking me some questions and that the other investigator was there to scribe. I was then asked to introduce myself and describe what my role was on the team. Once the introductions were out of the way, the lead investigator began to ask me about my working relationships with members of my team. He strategically asked about team members that he knew that I had no issues with first. Next, he began to ask about my working relationships with the pot-stirrers. There was an obvious shift in my demeanor at the mention of any of the pot-stirrers' names, and the lead investigator instantly noticed.

Lead investigator: "Your demeanor has changed; why is that?"

Me: "Because I'm really sad that it has had to come to this."

Lead investigator: "What do you mean?"

Me: "Aren't you here to discuss the ethics complaint that I filed a few weeks ago?"

The puzzled look on both of the investigators' faces let me know that they had absolutely no clue what I was referring to. Yes, you guessed it, I had just returned fire in this battle, and I struck the seemingly well-prepared internal investigators with a surprise plot twist.

Let me take a moment to bring you up to speed in regards to the plot twist that I just mentioned. In some of my previous chapters, I described how miserable I was while under attack. I also stated in earlier chapters that at one time, things were so bad for me in the workplace that I would drive to work in silence so that I could pray. What I did not reveal in earlier chapters are the instructions that God provided to me during this warfare battle.

The instructions that God provided me were simple. He instructed me to research and become familiar with my company's corporate policies. God also instructed me to research federal employment laws. In addition to the research, God also instructed me to write more detailed entries in my personal log of events notebook. After my research, I then knew that what was I was experiencing in the workplace was not normal, and in fact, it could be illegal. Under the guidance of the Holy Spirit, I spoke with my supervisor and manager to give them the opportunity to address my concerns. After a sufficient amount of time had passed and the behavior from the pot-stirrers had not changed, I then decided to file a formal complaint with the corporate internal investigations team.

Since I have now brought you up to speed on the surprise plot twist, let's get back to the investigation. After I disclosed to the investigators that I had also filed an internal ethics complaint against the pot-stirrers, the investigators let me know that they were unaware of my complaint. My complaint had not yet been assigned to an investigator as of yet, but I did have a copy of my submission.

In order to stay on task, the lead investigator stated that we would discuss the complaint against me first, and then we could discuss the complaint that I filed. I answered all of the questions truthfully. The lead investigator asked about my moment of frustration where I yelled at my team member. I admitted my wrongdoing and stated that I apologized to her twice, once verbally and another in writing. I also let the investigators know that my apology was accepted, and my working relationship with that particular team member was still intact. The lead investigator accepted my response and moved on.

The next set of questions from the lead investigator was

somewhat confusing to me. I was being asked about who I go to lunch with every day. That question was a little confusing to me because I knew that who I spent my personal time with should not be of any concern in a workplace investigation. The lead investigator asked that question because he was trying to determine if the specific complaint against me was true or not. Whew, nothing could have ever prepared me for the moment when the lead investigator revealed what the specific complaint against me was. I was being accused of being a racist workplace bully. Someone actually wrote in a statement that I was a racist workplace bully. I could not believe my ears.

After finding out what I was being accused of, I sat in silence for a moment because I was utterly shocked and appalled. Both of the investigators gazed at me intensely as I repeatedly shook my head in disgust. In all my life, I had never been falsely accused of something so horrible, something so degrading to my character, something that, if were true, could result in me being fired from my job. In that moment of silence, I remember feeling hurt because this was a low blow, but I maintained my composure because I knew that I was innocent, and the false accusations proved to me that the enemy was desperate to take me out.

Now that the specific complaint against me had been revealed, it was now time for me to defend myself and prove my innocence. My first rebuttal was in regards to the workplace bully accusation. I informed the investigator that the only example that was provided of my alleged workplace bully behavior was the one moment of frustration that I had with a fellow team member, and she and I resolved that issue on our own. I further stated to the investigators that one incident is hardly enough to display a pattern that could label me as a workplace bully. The lead investigator agreed.

My next and most important rebuttal was in regards to being accused of being a racist. I was accused of being racist because I allegedly only went to lunch with Black people, thus, the reason the lead investigator asked who I went to lunch with on most days. As silly as that accusation sounds, I still had to defend myself against it. I instructed the investigators to pull my instant message conversations from my computer to see where the same few people contacted me daily to see if I wanted to join them for lunch. I also told the investigators that they would not find any evidence of the pot-stirrers ever inviting me to lunch, nor would they find evidence of any non-Black person inviting me to lunch, and I turned them down. The lead investigator wrote down his last few notes and then said that we could now move on to discuss the complaint that I submitted.

Before we moved on to discuss my complaint, I asked the investigators if I could be excused to go retrieve the copy of my complaint that I submitted and my log of events notebooks. A few moments later, I rejoined the investigators in the small conference room. I first presented the copy of the ethics complaint that I submitted weeks prior. I also had printed copies of emails that I knew would be useful to the investigation. I sat quietly as the investigators read through my complaint. I then handed over my log of events notebook and the printed emails. My notebook was filled with detailed accounts of events that occurred within the department going back as far as two years. Each log entry included the date, time, participants, and nearby witnesses. As the lead investigator flipped through the pages of my log of events notebook, the expression on his face led me to believe that he was impressed by my record keeping. I sat calmly as I watched him peruse the pages of my log of events. I knew that I possessed evidence that would disprove all of the false accusations against me. When the lead investigator was finished glancing over my notes, he asked that I scan and email a copy of the notes over to him the following morning so that he could complete his investigation. At the conclusion of the meeting, the lead investigator thanked me for my time and also thanked me for making his job easier because of my excellent record keeping. I said my goodbyes and exited the conference room.

By God's grace, I was able to maintain my composure from the moment that I found out that I was the subject of an internal investigation, but my drive home was a different story. On my drive home from work after the investigation meeting, I was physically shaken and experienced a various array of emotions. I was angry, hurt, sad, and shocked. As soon as I entered my apartment, the hurt and sadness took over as tears fell from my eyes. As I sat on my couch and sobbed, all I could do was ask God how can some people be so evil to make up vicious, character assassinating lies about me? God did not immediately provide the answers to the questions that I was seeking. However, God did grant me peace to get through the rest of that night.

Although the investigation was supposed to be discreet, word had spread throughout the office. I received several phone calls and texts from coworkers that evening. Some of those who reached out were genuinely concerned about me and wanted to offer their moral support, while others only reached out to be nosey. Either way, I knew that no matter how I felt, I had to put on a brave face when I returned to the office the next morning.

The next morning, I was refreshed, and my spirit was renewed because I knew that God had my back. I did not deviate from my normal morning routine; I drove in silence all the way to work so that I could pray and talk to God. After the mentally draining day that I had endured one day before, I knew that I needed God's covering more than anything.

As usual, I was one of the first employees to arrive at the office. My early arrival gave me a chance to go to the restroom and check my facial expressions. I did not want to display even the smallest amount of resentment because I knew that all eyes would be on me that day. I gave myself one last pep talk and exited the restroom with a bright smile on my face and with my head held high. There was an obvious hint of arrogance in the atmosphere that radiated from the pot-stirrers, but I refused to react to it. There were people gathered in corners whispering, but I refused to allow it to affect me. Instead, I greeted everyone, even the pot-stirrers, with a genuine smile and a warm good morning. I even indulged in a little small talk that morning. Soon after, I began to email the requested information to the investigators. Once I completed the request, I continued my work day as usual. Confident in the fact that the outcome of the investigation was in God's trustworthy hands.

Do Not Submit to Your Feelings

When you experience warfare that includes false accusations, know that you are in good company. Jesus, King David, and the Apostle Paul were all falsely accused of wrongdoings, but they did not allow their feelings to discourage them. Your feelings are unreliable; therefore, when you are experiencing workplace warfare, it is important that you do not trust your feelings. Feelings can be fatal. Submitting to your feelings when you are under attack can kill your character, kill important relationships, and kill your decision-making capability. The enemy loves when you are in your feelings because your rationale is obscured, and that opens the door for him to come in and influence you to sin.

Rely on God's Strength

God is fully aware that when experiencing workplace warfare that you may not always feel as strong as you should. Relying on God's strength is the only way to overcome the battles that you will face. When you feel your spirit weakening, the first thing you should do is remind yourself that as a follower of Christ, you will never have to face any situation alone. It is also important for you to admit to God that you are weak. By admitting to God that you are weak, He then can come in and be strong for you. Additionally, you can quickly regain your spiritual strength by reading God's truth in His Word. Romans 12:2 tells us,

> Do not conform to the pattern of this world, but be transformed by the renewing of your mind. Then you will be able to test and approve what God's will is—his good, pleasing and perfect will.

Romans 12:2 (NIV)

The essential statement in this particular verse is "renewing your mind." The Word of God will renew your mind and, as a result, strengthen your spirit.

Vindication Is Connected to Integrity

Unwarranted attacks that involve false accusations can be especially trying, but God wants you to call out to Him to vindicate you. I would be remiss in my purpose if I did not tell you that your request for God to vindicate you must be founded on integrity. God wants to showcase to the world His love and faithfulness through you, but He cannot do that if you are not walking in integrity. Should you ever find yourself in an unfortunate situation where you are being falsely accused, take the time to examine yourself and ask God to examine your heart as well to make sure that you are not, in fact, guilty of what you are being accused of. Once you have examined yourself and God has examined your heart, you can then go before God as King David did in Psalm 35:24 (NKJV), "Vindicate me, O LORD my God, according to Your righteousness; And let them not rejoice over me."

Biblical Perspective

Throughout the Bible, there are many examples of where God vindicates his people. One of my favorite vindications is the story of King Saul versus David in the Book of 1 Samuel. The Prophet Samuel was instructed by God to anoint Saul as ruler over Israel. The Spirit of the Lord then came upon him. Initially, Saul was viewed as a good king because He obeyed God and led the Israelites to many battle victories. In chapter 13 of the Book of 1 Samuel, King Saul disobeys

God's commands, and the Prophet Samuel tells him that his reign will come to an end and that God will appoint another to be king of Israel.

The Lord then instructs Samuel to fill his flask with oil and go to Bethlehem to find a man named Jesse because He has selected one of his sons to be the next ruler of Israel. Samuel did as he was told and traveled to Bethlehem. Jesse was the father of eight sons, but God assured Samuel that He would let him know which one He has chosen to be the next king. Jesse presented seven of his sons at first, but none of them was the chosen one. Samuel then asked Jesse whether he had any more sons. Jesse said that he has one more son, his youngest son David who was out in the fields tending to the sheep and goats. It is estimated that David was approximately fifteen years old at this time. Samuel sent for David. As soon as David arrived, the Lord told Samuel that he was the one and Samuel anointed David's head with oil, and the Spirit of the Lord was upon David from that day on.

Now that the Spirit of the Lord was no longer in Saul, he was often tormented and restless. Saul instructed his servants to find a musician to play soothing music for him when his spirit was troubling him. One of the servants suggested David because he just so happens to be an excellent harp player. David is summoned to play music for Saul. Saul quickly became quite fond of David and requested that Jesse allow him to remain with him.

Over the years, David was an excellent servant to Saul, and he also grew to be a mighty warrior. (We should all know the story of how David defeated the giant Philistine Goliath. If you are not familiar with the story of David and Goliath, it is detailed in 1 Samuel, chapter 17.) After his defeat of Goliath, David became a high-ranking official in Saul's army. He was successful on any mission that Saul sent him on. David was such a great warrior that people began to celebrate him, and this made Saul angry and jealous. Saul also began to fear that David would take his kingdom from him.

Saul's anger, fear, and jealousy have caused him to want David killed, although David had not done anything wrong. First, Saul attempted to kill David himself by hurling his spear towards him, but David was able to dodge the spear. Saul then started plotting on ways to get David killed in war, but because God was with David, Saul was unsuccessful in his attempts. Next, Saul ordered his son Jonathan and all of his servants to kill David. Fortunately for David, Jonathan was his best friend and told him of his father's desire to have him killed; David was forced to go on the run. Of course, David is distressed because he has no idea why a king that he loves suddenly wants him killed. Every place that Saul heard that David visited, he sent his men there in hopes of killing David. He searched daily. David, in the meantime, had assembled a small army of men.

One day as Saul and his men were in pursuit of David, Saul went into a cave to relieve himself. He was unaware that David and his men were hiding in that same cave. David's men urged him to take this opportunity to kill Saul. Instead, David quietly crept up behind Saul and cut off a corner of his robe with his sword. David's act was unnoticed by Saul. When Saul was finished, he exited the cave, and David exited the cave right after him. Once outside of the cave, David announced himself to Saul. David then tells Saul that he has no intention of doing him any harm, although he could have killed him moments ago. He proved what he was saying by showing Saul the piece of the robe that he cut from his hem while they were inside the cave. Saul then became emotional and started to cry as he realized that David chose to show him kindness and mercy by not killing him when he had the chance to. At that moment, Saul ended his pursuit to kill David.

Battle Summary

It is impossible for you to submit to God and your feelings at the same time. If you make the decision to listen to your feelings, you will hinder your ability to hear God. Whenever you are under attack, you have to get out of your feelings and get into prayer. When I initially found out that I was under investigation, of course, I was upset and afraid. Who would not be? If I had submitted to and dwelled on those feelings of anger and fear, I would not have heard God when he instructed me to go to my car and pray. Had I submitted to my feelings during the investigation meeting, I would not have been able to maintain my composure which proved to be vital when I had to present my truth.

Contrary to my decision not to submit my feelings, Saul did submit to his feelings. Shortly after Saul submitted to his feelings of contempt towards David, the irrational decisions soon followed. Unfortunately for Saul, when he submitted to his feelings, he further separated himself from God.

As detailed in Scripture, David could have easily repaid Saul's evil with evil, but he instead stood firm on his faith in God. Saul gathered many men to join him to hunt David, but David never lost his focus, and he was eventually vindicated and went on to be a great king and military leader over Israel. So always keep in mind that when faced with warfare, you have two choices; focus on who is against you or focus on the mighty God who is with you.

Workplace Warfare Tips

- When you operate in your feelings, the enemy can operate in you.

- When you call for vindication, make sure it is rooted in integrity.

- Ill-willed motives remove God's covering.

A Scripture to Ponder

"Fear not, for I *am* with you; Be not dismayed, for I *am* your God. I will strengthen you, Yes, I will help you, I will uphold you with My righteous right hand" (Isaiah 41:10, NKJV).

CHAPTER SIX

Victory Is Declared

No matter how fierce the enemy seems—when fear cripples us, anger enrages us, or selfishness possesses us; when adversity crushes us, opposition hounds us, or temptation plagues us—God is greater.

—Katy Kauffman

It had now been a few weeks since the investigation meeting. The pot-stirrers were on their best behavior due to the fact that the outcome of the investigation was still pending. I, too, had made it a point to be extra kind and sociable, not because I was afraid of what the outcome of the investigation would be, but because I was confident in what the outcome would be. Although I was confident that God would vindicate me, I was also anxious for this battle to come to an end.

One day I received a meeting request from the department manager. The meeting request did not have an entry in the subject line, so that was an indicator that this meeting would likely discuss a private matter. When I arrived at my manager's office, my supervisor was also in attendance. That was the moment that I realized that the pending investigation had been resolved, and this was the meeting to discuss the outcome. Once I sat down, my manager confirmed what I was thinking; this was indeed the meeting to discuss the outcome of the investigation. I was not nervous at all. I listened intensely as my manager discussed the findings. After he rambled on for minutes, he finally revealed that there were no findings against me! I silently thanked God as I exited my manager's office. God had once again shown Himself faithful in my life.

In addition to being totally vindicated, there was an added surprise that came about as a result of the investigation against me. I soon found out that due to some of the information that I recorded in my log of events notebook, an additional investigation into the queen pot-stirrer was initiated. The queen pot-stirrer, whom I later found out was the one who submitted the false allegations against me, would now face disciplinary action for the derogatory behavior that she often displayed in the workplace.

Remain Humble in the Jungle

Throughout this book, I have discussed how warfare in itself is tough to go through; but when the warfare has high visibility, it makes it even more nerve-wracking to endure. Your enemies are waiting and watching to see if their attacks will destroy you as they hoped they would. The unbelievers are waiting and watching to see if your God will deliver you from evil as He promised. And lastly, your supporters are waiting and watching to see if you will be victorious or not. With so many people awaiting the outcome, you may be tempted to flaunt your victory in front of your enemies once the battle is over. Scripture tells us in James 4:6 (NKJV), "God resists the proud, But gives grace to the humble." So, before you stick out your tongue and taunt your enemies, remember that God honors humility. The world may view humility as weakness, but your father in Heaven sees humility as a strength.

Biblical Perspective

An old adage that I have heard many times throughout my life says, "When you did one grave, you better dig two." Translated, that adage means that when you're hypothetically plotting and preparing for the death of someone else, you need to prepare for your own death as well. In the Bible, the Book of Esther has a story that embodies this old adage.

Esther was a beautiful young Jewish woman who was chosen to be queen by the Persian King Xerxes. Esther's cousin Mordecai advised Esther not to reveal to the king that she was of Jewish heritage, so she did as she was told. Soon after Esther was chosen as queen, Mordecai foiled an assassination plot against King Xerxes. From then on, the king favored Mordecai, and he was also named as an official within the empire.

Sometime later, King Xerxes appointed a man named Haman as the top official in the empire. Haman expected all of the other officials to bow down in reverence to him each time he passed by, but Mordecai refused to do so. Of course, this angered Haman. When Haman learned that Mordecai was Jewish, he then decided that all Jewish people in the kingdom should be destroyed because of Mordecai's refusal to bow to him. His next course of action was to meet with King Xerxes and present his plan.

When Haman met with King Xerxes, he knew that he would have to stretch the truth in order to succeed in his evil plans. Haman told King Xerxes that the Jewish people throughout the kingdom refused to obey the king's commands, and it was not in the king's best interest to let any of the Jewish people live. King Xerxes was persuaded by Haman to issue a decree to destroy all Jewish people starting in March of the following year. What neither Haman nor King Xerxes knew at the time is that they were also issuing a death decree for their beloved Queen Esther.

When Mordecai heard of the newly issued decree, he immediately went into mourning for himself and all of his Jewish people. When Queen Esther heard that her cousin Mordecai was in mourning, she sent her attendants to him to find out why he was in mourning. Mordecai sent a copy of the newly issued decree back to Queen Esther and asked for her help to prevent the destruction of the Jewish people amongst the kingdom. After several back-and-forth messages between Esther and Mordecai, Esther gave instructions for all of the Jewish people, including herself, to fast for three days as she prepared to go before her husband, King Xerxes. Although Esther was the queen, she knew that going before King Xerxes without being summoned could possibly mean an immediate death for her; however, she was willing to take this risk to hopefully save her people from pending destruction. When Esther approached King Xerxes, he held out his golden scepter. This gesture meant that he would not do her any harm, although she approached him without a summons. Esther then asked King Xerxes if she could prepare a banquet for him and Haman so that she could present her official request; King Xerxes then agreed.

Meanwhile, as Esther and Mordecai strategized in an attempt to save the Jewish people, Haman, on the other hand, continued to plot Mordecai's death. Haman bragged to his wife and friends about his invite to a private dinner banquet. He then instructed his wife and his friends to erect a seventy-five-foot sharpened pole and planned on asking King Xerxes the next day to impale Mordecai on that pole.

During the private banquet that Queen Esther arranged, King Xerxes spoke, "Tell me what you want, Queen Esther. What is your request? I will give it to you, even if it is half the kingdom!" (Esther 7:2, NLT). Queen Esther then asked the king that he spare her life and the lives of her people. King Xerxes was confused and wanted to know who would dare threaten to do harm to his queen. It was then that Esther revealed that she was of Jewish descent and that Haman intended on doing her and her people harm. The blood immediately drained from Haman's face as he learned that Queen Esther was of Jewish heritage. Haman knew that the king would surely kill him. Moments later, King Xerxes ordered his men to impale Haman on the same sharpened pole that he had set up to kill Mordecai.

Battle Summary

Haman and the queen pot-stirrer who falsely accused me definitely had a few things in common. They both decided at some point in time that the person they hated deserved to be destroyed, and it was solely up to them to make it happen. They both plotted and schemed down the most minuscule details in hopes of destroying their adversaries. Neither one of them ever stopped for a moment to consider if their adversary was protected by God. That lack of consideration proved to be a huge mistake in both situations. The outcome of both situations demonstrated that you cannot be victorious in a battle, no matter how contrived your efforts are, when your opponent is backed by God.

Workplace Warfare Tips

- The presence of humility means the absence of pride.

- Before you plot against them, consider who they serve.

- God's team is always the winning team.

A Scripture to Ponder

"My experience shows that those who plant trouble and cultivate evil will harvest the same" (Job 4:8, NLT).

SECTION III:
LIFE AFTER
THE BATTLE

"Don't repay evil for evil. Don't retaliate with insults when people insult you. Instead, pay them back with a blessing. That is what God has called you to do, and he will grant you his blessing" (1 Peter 3:9, NLT).

CHAPTER SEVEN

You've Triumphed, Now What?

*To me, it has been a source of great comfort and
strength in the day of battle, just to remember that
the secret of steadfastness, and indeed, of victory,
is the recognition that "the Lord is at hand.*

—Duncan Campbell

After I was cleared in the investigation, I felt like I could finally breathe again. Although my team appeared to have returned to some sort of normalcy, I knew that it was all superficial, but I refused to overthink things and went along with however things flowed. What I was most thankful for was that the attacks from the pot-stirrers against me had ceased, and I was no longer experiencing anxiety. Sadly, I noticed that others in the department were the target of their now subtle attacks. Yes, drama had calmed down significantly, but I knew deep down I had outgrown the department, so I then began to search, apply, and interview for human resources roles outside of the Human Resources Shared Services Center. In the meantime, I had to be strong and endure.

As the workload increased for the team, my supervisor

decided to bring in a contractor to help us out. I did not have much interaction with this contractor, so I did not know too much about her personality or her work ethic. One day the pot-stirrers asked me to meet with them in a private conference. The purpose of the meeting was that they all had issues with the contractor. They proceeded to detail their frustrations to me. As they went on, I thought to myself, *Why are they telling me all of these things?* They then told me that they planned on meeting with our supervisor in hopes of getting the contractor fired. They even asked me if I wanted to attend the meeting with them! This same group of women who conspired in an attempt to get me fired just a few months ago was now trying to recruit me to help them get someone else fired. The pot-stirrers even knew that I did not have enough interactions with the contractor to provide a truthful opinion to our supervisor, but they did not care. All they cared about was succeeding in their plans and wanted additional allies. I was appalled, but I managed to maintain my poker face. I wanted absolutely nothing to do with their scheme, so I did not attend their meeting with our supervisor. Unfortunately, the pot-stirrers' plans succeeded this time, and the contractor was fired.

Not long after the contractor was fired, our office began renovations to make our cubicles larger. Due to the renovations, I was assigned to move into the cubicle that was previously occupied by the now-fired contractor. As I was cleaning out the desk's drawers, I discovered a notebook.

I started to just toss the notebook in the trash, but my spirit led me to open it. After reading a few sentences, I became paralyzed with shock and disbelief. What I was reading was the fired contractor's log of events that detailed how she and the pot-stirrers were plotting to initiate warfare on me again. I was furious. I stormed out of the department and into the conference room for some privacy while I gathered my thoughts. After I stewed in my anger for a few minutes, God reminded me that He blocked it. In fact, the weapon that they were forming did not prosper against me. The weapon actually backfired on the contractor. With that revelation from God, I instantly calmed down. I went back into the department, and I shredded the pages of the contractor's notebook. Shredding the notebook pages was sort of symbolic to me. As I shredded each page, I released the anger because God had protected me from my enemies yet again. To my knowledge, the pot-stirrers never knew that I had discovered the notebook.

Battles Have a Purpose

Rest assured that any battle that God allows, He has a specific purpose for it. As I mentioned in chapter one, no one is exempt from warfare; therefore, when you experience battles, it is not necessarily the result of you being disobedient. For full transparency, God will discipline those He loves due to disobedience, but not every trial in life is a punishment. There are countless reasons why God will allow warfare in your life; I will provide you with a few examples.

God desires for you to be totally dependent on Him. Typically, the first response to adversity is to try and figure out how you can solve it on your own. Next, you may seek advice from another person or source, but God wants you to come to Him first. Honestly, it is quite offensive to God when you seek others before you seek Him. As you begin to cast your cares unto God, He will then begin to release strategy to you and also point you in the direction of the wise counsel that He has assigned to help you. Victory in your warfare proves to others that God is dependable.

When God wants you to grow spiritually, He will sometimes allow you to experience warfare. Spiritual growth can include but is not limited to: increasing your knowledge and understanding of God and His Word, increasing your faith in God, and walking in obedience to God. When you are in the midst of a battle, and you read a few verses in your Bible or another Christian self-help book, and you begin to feel at peace, that is a for sure sign that you are growing spiritually. Increased faith is another obvious indicator that you are growing spiritually. The popular saying, "Faith is like a muscle, you have to strengthen it in order for it to grow," is very true, so it should come as no surprise that you must experience some trials in order to increase your faith. If there were no trials in life, there would be no opportunities for you to display your trust in God.

The enemy is not very creative; he has been using the same types of warfare to attack God's people since the beginning of time. With that said, God will sometimes allow you to go through a battle so that you can be the person He assigns to help someone else when they experience the same type of warfare in the future. Throughout the years, God has used me on many occasions to help others while they are in the midst of workplace warfare. My personal experience taught me that the warfare that I experienced was for my personal benefit and the benefit of others.

What Did the Battle Teach or Reveal to You?

You have triumphed in the battle, and now it is time to move on. Do not move on without first assessing the lessons learned and acknowledging the revelations from the battle. Battles can be some of our most influential teachers. When you assess the lessons that you have learned as a result of your battle, you will gain knowledge that you can utilize for the rest of your life. In some cases, your lesson learned may be for you to be more discerning because being too trusting too fast can leave you vulnerable to an attack. A battle can reveal to you if there are any personal changes that you should make to prevent you from being a warfare target in the future. And most importantly, a battle can reveal who is truly for you and who is secretly against you.

Biblical Perspective

The best and the most well-known example in the Bible of a battle having a specific purpose is in the Book of Matthew with the story of the trial and crucifixion of Jesus. Jesus was sent to earth on assignment by God to save mankind from their sins. Once Jesus was baptized, the Holy Spirit came upon him, and he then began his preaching ministry.

All throughout his ministry, Jesus preached the Gospel, healed the sick, raised the dead, fed the hungry, and forgave sins. Even with all of the miracles that Jesus performed, some of the religious leaders were not impressed, nor did they believe that he was the Messiah, and as a result, warfare was initiated. As the story is told in the Book of Matthew, chapters 26 and 27, Jesus was falsely accused, betrayed by a close friend, and arrested. After Jesus' arrest, he was tried and convicted of those false charges and went on to suffer a brutal public crucifixion. Do not be mistaken; as the son of God, Jesus could have decided not to endure the battle, but he understood his assignment. By suffering a horrible death that was witnessed by many, then rising from the dead three days later proved that Jesus was truly the Messiah sent to earth by God to save mankind.

Battle Summary

Imagine what our world would be like today had Jesus

allowed the pain that he experienced to deter him from fulling his assignment. The pain and humiliation that you may experience during warfare can easily prevent you from remembering that there is a purpose in the battle. Sometimes God will reveal to you early on the specific purpose of the battle that you are facing, and in other times the purpose may be revealed to you later on in life. You may not always understand the purpose of the battles that you face but rest assured that there is a purpose indeed. The Bible tells you in Isaiah 55:8 (NKJV), "For My thoughts *are not your thoughts. Nor are your ways My ways," says the* LORD."

With that scripture noted, the next time you are in the midst of a battle, regardless of how intense it is, take a moment to praise God and acknowledge that all battles are accompanied by a purpose.

Workplace Warfare Tips

- Warfare may be painful, but it is always purposeful.

- Earnestly seek God and ask Him to reveal all that you need to know.

A Scripture to Ponder

> "Many are the plans in a person's heart, but it is the LORD's purpose that prevails" (Proverbs 19:21, NIV).

CHAPTER EIGHT

Final Thoughts

*As you walk in God's divine wisdom, you will
surely begin to see a greater measure of victory
and good success in your life.*

—Joseph Prince

I remained in the Human Resources Shared Services Center until I was selected for a promotion to the company's corporate office. Prior to being selected for the promotion, I still worked on the same team as the pot-stirrers. After the dust completely settled, I had no other issues with any of them. Some minor annoyances popped up here and there, but I was completely unbothered because I made the decision to forgive all of them for everything that they did to me.

Forgiveness Frees Y-O-U

Some of you may now be wondering how I could work peacefully in the same office with the same people who tried to destroy me. It is simple; I chose forgiveness over bitterness.

In today's society, many people obtain their personal opinions and viewpoints from social media and other people that they admire. Unfortunately, this trend has caused many people to misunderstand and misinterpret what forgiveness truly is. For example, if the family of a murder victim decides to forgive the murderer, those who do not truly know what forgiveness means will lash out at the family. That is a clear indication that the true biblical interpretation of forgiveness has been lost. Allow me to take this opportunity to clear up a few misinterpretations of forgiveness.

The first misinterpretation of forgiveness that I would like to clear up is that when you decide to forgive someone, that does not mean that you are telling the offender that you are okay with the offense that they have committed. Secondly, you do not have to restore relationships with someone when you decide to forgive them. It is your individual choice to restore a relationship with your offender once you have forgiven them. Thirdly, forgiving someone who has offended you does not have to happen immediately. God is quite aware that some offenses are far too great to be forgiven immediately. Forgiveness is a process. Lastly, when you decide to forgive someone, that does not mean that you want them to forgo the consequences of their actions. I intentionally used the term "decide" because forgiving someone is a decision you make, not a feeling that you have toward the offender or the offense.

Now that I have cleared up a few misconceptions in regards to forgiveness, I now want you to understand how forgiveness frees you. Matthew 6:15 (NIV) tells us, "But if you do not forgive others their sins, your Father will not forgive your sins." With that said, understand that God requires us to forgive others in order for Him to forgive us of the sins that we commit. This is major; this means that God calls us to forgive others. Understand that there will be many times throughout your life that you will have to forgive people who do not care that they have offended you or they do not know that they have offended you, but choose to forgive them anyway.

I want you to think of a time in your past when you have done something that you knew was wrong or a time when you have offended someone. Now I want you to imagine God not forgiving you for what you have done because you are holding on to unforgiveness towards someone else. Ouch. God will sometimes postpone your blessings because you are holding on to unforgiveness. It is almost scary to think about not receiving a blessing that you have been praying and fasting for because you are carrying unforgiveness in your heart. With that said, I think you would agree with me when I say that holding on to unforgiveness is just not worth it.

When someone commits an offense against you, it hurts you and angers you. According to Mayo Clinic, anger causes your heart rate and blood pressure to increase; thus, when you forgive someone, you free yourself from physical distress by casting your anger and hurt onto God. Again, forgiving your offenders is not releasing them of their responsibility for the offense; it is freeing yourself from the hurt and anger that it has caused you.

From Saul to Paul

Many of you may be familiar with the story of God converting a Pharisee named Saul into the Apostle Paul. Let me give you a refresher. Saul was once a persecutor of those who believed in Jesus. However, while Saul was on his way to Damascus to persecute and arrest believers, God converted him into a believer. Soon after, Saul's name was changed to Paul, and he went on to write most of the New Testament in the Bible. I provided this refresher of the conversion of the Apostle Paul to prove that the same God that changed a man who once killed and jailed Christians into one of the most important authors in the Bible can also change your coworkers who once initiated workplace warfare on you. Not all your coworkers will be changed, but let this example serve as a reminder that even the worst of the worst can be changed by God. For the ones that do not change, I recommend that you continue to walk in love. Proverbs 16:7 (NKJV) says, "When a man's ways please the LORD, He makes even his enemies to be at peace with him."

Romans 8:28

In the words of the esteemed Prophetess Tera Carissa Hodges, "Attacks may be painful, but they are always purposeful." I could not agree with this statement any more. In many cases, people will stress over the agony that the battle is causing before they consider how the battle is working for their good. I am guilty of doing this same thing many times. That is why it is so important to read and meditate on the scriptures to acquire an understanding of God's truth. The Bible tells us in Romans 8:28 (NKJV), "And we know that all things work together for good to those who love God, to those who are the called according to *His* purpose." Take note that the scripture does not say that some things work together for your good; it says that *all* things work together for your good. So, the next time you are in the midst of a battle, I insist that you shift your focus from the pain of the battle to the purpose of the battle. Seek God and ask Him how the warfare is working for your good.

Conclusion

The workplace warfare that I detailed throughout this book is not the only warfare that I have ever experienced in the workplace, but it was by far the most intense. This workplace warfare that I described was so intense that, at times, I became extremely emotional as I was writing and recollecting my experience. Although the battle was intense,

I truly have grown to appreciate what I went through at that time because the spiritual growth and wisdom that I gained as a result of it far outweigh the traumatic experience that I endured at that time. When I experience workplace warfare in my current role, I think back on that experience and tap into the wisdom that I obtained from it. I first remind myself that the battle is spiritual and not to take the warfare personally. I then remember to seek God for guidance and strategy so that I can have His peace throughout the battle. And lastly, I give myself grace when, and if, I allow my flesh to prevail over my spirit.

It is a well-known fact that we spend most of our time in the workplace; therefore, it should come as no surprise that the workplace is a frequent battleground for so much spiritual warfare. I have confidence that the details of my warfare and triumph will inspire others to have the courage to stand up against the enemy when he initiates warfare for many years to come. Ephesians 6:16 (NIV) says, "In addition to all this, take up the shield of faith, with which you can extinguish all the flaming arrows of the evil one." Ultimately, I hope this book has fulfilled God's intended purpose of increasing awareness of warfare within the workplace and providing knowledge on how to overcome it. Stand firm in your faith and stay connected to God so that He can lead you to victory time and time again.

The End

Bonus: Spiritual Weapons for Workplace Warfare

Workplace warfare has been initiated against you, and you have decided that you will not just lie down and take it. Your plan is to trust God to help you fight your way to victory, but you do not know exactly where to start. Check out my top three spiritual weapons that help me overcome workplace warfare below.

1. Prayer and Meditation

Prayer and meditation are always going to be your most powerful weapons when faced with workplace warfare. Prayer allows for you to go before God with your situation and seek Him for guidance. Meditation allows for you to sit still before God and await His instructions.

2. Fasting

Fasting is another powerful and effective weapon to defend yourself against workplace warfare. Fasting is used in combination with focused prayer directed towards your situation. Deliverance and breakthroughs come about as a result of fasting.

3. Seed Sowing

Many people only equate seed sowing to financial break-throughs, but there is more to it than that. Sowing financial seeds in the midst of workplace warfare can also bring about protection, favor, and breakthroughs in your situation.

ABOUT THE AUTHOR

Courtni Michelle is a human resources professional with thirteen years of experience in corporate settings. She holds a Bachelor's and Master's degree in Business Administration, both with concentrations in Human Resources Management. Courtni currently works and resides in the Houston, Texas, area.

CPSIA information can be obtained
at www.ICGtesting.com
Printed in the USA
LVHW080537180422
716440LV00014BB/1090